DATE DUE

Texas v. Johnson

The Flag-Burning Case

J. Anthony Miller

Landmark Supreme Court Cases

Enslow Publishers, Inc.

40 Industrial Road   PO Box 38
Box 398   Aldershot
Berkeley Heights, NJ 07922   Hants GU12 6BP
USA   UK

http://www.enslow.com

Library of Congress Cataloging-in-Publication Data

Miller, J. Anthony.
    Texas v. Johnson: the flag-burning case / J. Anthony Miller.
        p. cm. — (Landmark Supreme Court cases)
    Includes bibliographical references and index.
    Summary: Covers the case of Texas v. Johnson, in which the question before the Court
was whether flag burning is an activity protected by the Bill of Rights.
    ISBN 0-89490-858-8
    1. Johnson, Gregory Lee—Trials, litigation, etc.—Juvenile literature. 2. Flags—
Desecration—United States—Juvenile literature. 3. Freedom of speech—United
States—Juvenile literature. 4. Dissenters—Legal status, laws, etc.—United States—
Juvenile literature. 5. Flags—Law and legislation—United States—Criminal
provisions—Juvenile literature. [1. Johnson, Gregory Lee—Trials, litigation, etc.
2. Flags—Desecration. 3. Freedom of speech.] I. Title II. Series.
KF224.J64M55   1997
342.73'0854—dc20
[347.302854]   96-34850
                                                            CIP
                                                            AC

Printed in the United States of America

10 9 8 7 6 5 4 3

Photo Credits: J. Anthony Miller, pp. 70, 76, 88; Kenneth Jarecke, 1990, p. 4;
National Archives, pp. 7, 11, 13, 23, 32, 39, 43, 48, 54, 60, 65, 73, 94, 96;
Official White House photo, p. 86; Smithsonian Institution, Dane Peland
photographer, courtesy of the Supreme Court of the United States, p. 81.

Cover Photo: J. Anthony Miller

Contents

Flag burning became a political issue during the 1984 Republican National Convention in Dallas, Texas.

1

New Patriotism and No Patriotism

"[R]ed, white and blue, we spit on you, you stand for plunder, you will go under."

"Reagan, Mondale which will it be? Either one means World War III."

"Ronald Reagan, killer of the hour, Perfect example of U.S. power."[1]

The crowd chanted loudly as it marched through the streets of Dallas, Texas. Dallas was the site of the 1984 Republican National Convention and the eyes of the nation were focused on it. The media would bring this important political event into millions of American living rooms.

Inside the convention hall, citizens from every state gathered to show support for their presidential candidate. A sea of people excitedly chanted political slogans, cheered, and waved hand-held American flags. They listened intently to the speeches of their favorite politicians.

Outside, a crowd of some one hundred angry demonstrators gathered to protest the policies of the Republican president and express their displeasure. They held "die-ins" in which they acted out death from nuclear war. They spray-painted walls and overturned potted plants. One protestor pulled down a flapping American flag from the glistening pole near the crowd. The chanters gathered near Gregory Lee ("Joey") Johnson, a member of the Revolutionary Communist Youth Brigade. They handed him the flag, the national symbol of liberty and democracy. Instead of saluting it, Johnson doused the flag with kerosene and set it ablaze. The crowd chanted, "America, the red, white, and blue, we spit on you."[2]

Many onlookers were shocked and offended by this disrespect for the symbol that American schoolchildren honor each morning. One of the spectators carefully gathered the charred remains of the flag for burial as an act of respect for the nation's symbol. Johnson was arrested for violating a Texas criminal law against destroying a respected object—in this case the American flag.

When Johnson went to trial, he claimed that his acts were political. He said that what he did was protected as

Legend says that George Washington and two representatives from Congress asked Betsy Ross to make the first flag of the United States. The thirteen stars and the thirteen stripes each represented the thirteen original colonies.

free speech under the Free Speech Clause of the First Amendment to the United States Constitution. It says: "Congress shall make no law . . . abridging the freedom of speech. . . ." Johnson believed that this meant that no law could stop him from speaking out against the United States government or from burning its flag in protest. Johnson explained the idea behind his method of expression:

> The American Flag was burned as Ronald Reagan was being renominated as President. And a more powerful statement of symbolic speech, whether you agree with it or not, couldn't have been made at that time. . . . We had new patriotism and no patriotism.[3]

Johnson was convicted, sentenced to one year in prison, and fined two thousand dollars. His case then began its climb to the United States Supreme Court. The Court of Appeals for the Fifth District of Texas at Dallas upheld his conviction, but the Texas Court of Criminal Appeals reversed it. That court, agreeing with Johnson, held that his conduct was symbolic speech protected by the First Amendment. When Johnson's case reached the United States Supreme Court, the highest rung of the judicial ladder, an important legal question was raised. The case, now known as *Texas* v. *Johnson,* asked: Can the federal government protect a symbol of political freedom by prohibiting the exercise of political freedom?

2

Political Dissent in the United States

The arrest of Joey Johnson for burning an American flag in a demonstration created a dilemma. On one hand, a person has the right to speak freely against the government. On the other hand, the government has control over its citizens' actions and speech. Tension results when a government's efforts to protect itself against criticism conflict with its citizens' desire to be critical of that government. This tension is shown in the history of the United States.

The early American colonists' disagreement and displeasure with the ruling English king led to the establishment of the United States. Thomas Jefferson wrote for the American colonists in the Declaration of

Independence. This document asserted the American colonists' independence and explained why they were breaking away from England's rule. Jefferson also wrote about the colonists' right to establish a new nation. When the Declaration of Independence was written in 1776, England was a powerful nation. England's King George III was one of the most politically powerful people in the world. The colonists, on the other hand, were not powerful and did not have a well-trained army or much money. They were simply people who believed that they were being mistreated. They wanted to speak out, to make their opinions known, but speaking against the English government was not allowed. Many colonists were put in prison for saying that the English were treating them unfairly. Newspaper articles critical of the English government were written and distributed throughout the colonies. The articles were signed "Publius," a false name that kept the writers' true identities secret. Thomas Jefferson and the other signers of the Declaration of Independence were bold and brave. By expressing their political beliefs, these men were risking severe punishment by the English king. They believed that King George had violated a bond, or agreement, with the colonists. England did not agree. The colonists' opinions, and the actions that followed, led to the American Revolutionary War.

The interior of Independence Hall in Philadelphia, Pennsylvania, is shown here. This is where the Founding Fathers declared our nation's independence from England.

After finally winning the hard-fought war against England, the colonies wanted to adopt a written constitution for their new government. A constitution is a document agreed upon by the people as the controlling law of the land. A constitution also describes the powers and limits of the government. The new American Constitution was adopted without a written statement of individual rights. The framers of the United States Constitution (those who wrote the Constitution) believed that a statement of individual rights was not necessary. Individual rights are the legal rights of individual citizens. The Constitution granted only limited rights to the federal government. So, the framers believed that the federal government could do only those things that were specifically written in the Constitution. The Constitution did not say that the federal government could, for example, interfere with free speech. So, they believed the government could not interfere with free speech. They feared that granting some specific rights to citizens could be interpreted to mean that the citizens had *only* those specific rights. Many citizens, however, were concerned that they would not have the right to publicly disagree with the new government. The new Constitution, after all, did not specifically grant the right to free speech. The citizens believed that they had certain "inalienable

The United States Constitution, as originally adopted, did not contain a statement of individual legal rights. The drafters believed that a statement of specific rights could be interpreted to limit the citizens' legal rights to only those rights expressly stated.

rights" (individual rights that could not be given away) with which the government simply could not interfere, even if they were not specifically written. The citizens of the new nation remembered that England had tried to prevent them from speaking and writing against the English government. They did not want to be fearful of the new government's power. Therefore, the people of the new country wanted some of their important individual legal rights written in a binding legal document. This would assure the protection of those rights against interference by the government. On September 25, 1789, the First Congress proposed twelve amendments or additions to the Constitution. The states accepted only ten of the proposed twelve amendments. Those ten amendments to the Constitution of the United States became known as the Bill of Rights. These amendments were intended to ensure certain undeniable freedoms for individuals. They also protected certain personal freedoms from federal government intrusion.

The First Amendment was adopted in 1791. It limited the federal government's power over an individual's rights to practice religion, to assemble with others, and to complain about the government. The First Amendment says:

> Congress shall make no law respecting an establishment of religion, or prohibiting the free exercise thereof; or abridging the freedom of speech, or of the press; or the right of the people peaceably to assemble, and to petition the Government for a redress of grievances.

Perhaps the most controversial part of the First Amendment is the Free Speech Clause, which says: "Congress shall make no law . . . abridging the freedom of speech. . . ." The meaning of this clause may seem clear. Congress—consisting of both the United States Senate and the House of Representatives—is not allowed to make any law that abridges (diminishes or reduces) a person's freedom of speech. But what does it mean legally? Does it mean that a person may say anything to anyone at any time and in any manner? For example, may a person lawfully yell obscene language at the top of his or her lungs into a loudspeaker in the middle of the night on the intensive care ward of a religious hospital? If not, then what are the limitations? What does this constitutional provision mean? To find out we must look to history and the legal cases that interpret its meaning.

During the early years of our country, the new government was insecure and determined to protect itself. Government leaders felt vulnerable to the influence of those who disagreed with the government's policies. Congress began enacting laws to regulate written, spoken, or published words that criticized the federal government. The Sedition Act of 1798, for example, made it a crime to write, utter, or publish:

> . . . any false, scandalous, and malicious writing . . . against the government of the United States, or either house of the Congress . . . or the President . . . with intent to defame [them] . . . or to bring them . . . into contempt or disrepute; or to excite against them . . . the hatred of the good people of the United States, or to stir up sedition within the United States, or to excite any unlawful combinations therein, for opposing or resisting any law of the United States, or any act of the President of the United States, done in pursuance of any such law, or of the powers in him vested by the Constitution of the United States, or to resist, oppose, or defeat any such law or act. . . .[1]

In effect it was against the law to write, speak, or publish anything against the federal government. The Sedition Act remained in effect until March 3, 1801, when it expired.

A similar law, the Espionage Act, was passed in 1917. It was changed in 1918 to make it a crime to say things "intended to bring the form of government of the United States into contempt, scorn, contumely, or disrepute." In other words, it was now a crime to speak out against the United States government. The United States used the Espionage Act to convict persons for encouraging soldiers to speak against their superior officers. It was in relation to this Act that the United States Supreme Court created an important standard for limitations on free speech.

In December 1917, a group of American citizens had been convicted of violating the Espionage Act.[2] The group had sent to young men being drafted, pamphlets that were intended to get in the way of military recruitment and enlistment. The case of *Schenck* v. *United States* reached the Supreme Court in 1919. Justice Oliver Wendell Holmes wrote the opinion for the Court. He created a free speech standard referred to as the "clear and present danger" test. This legal test says that, when the Court is determining if speech is constitutionally protected, it must decide whether the words create an imminent danger that must be legally prevented. If the words, taken as a whole, create a situation that would violate a valid state or federal law, then the words are not legally protected. If the words do not constitute a risk of causing unlawful action, then the Free Speech Clause protects the person who speaks them. The government also has the authority to prevent a person from taking up arms against it. It does not, however, have the right to prevent a person from talking about taking up arms against the government. The question, then, is whether the words create a "clear and present danger" of unlawful action. Justice Holmes defined the "clear and present danger" test in his opinion, saying:

> We admit that in many places and in ordinary times the defendants, in saying all that was said in the circular, would have been within their constitutional rights. But the character of every act depends upon the circumstances in which it is done. . . . The most stringent protection of free speech would not protect a man in falsely shouting fire in a theater, and causing a panic. . . . The question in every case is whether the words used are used in such circumstances and are of such a nature as to create a clear and present danger that they will bring about the substantive evils that Congress has a right to prevent. It is a question of proximity and degree.[3]

Justice Holmes believed that the words in the pamphlets *did* create a real danger of causing unlawful action. The convictions were upheld.

Nearly forty years later, in 1957, in *Yates* v. *United States,* the Supreme Court reviewed the case of fourteen persons convicted of violating a federal law, the Smith Act, for supporting Communism and the overthrow of the United States.[4] The Court found that the only evidence was that the defendants believed in and talked about their opinions favoring the overthrow of the government. However, there was no evidence that they had encouraged anyone to actually overthrow the government. Their speech was thus protected, and the convictions were reversed.

The *Yates* case dealt with a federal law and not a state law. As late as 1922, the Supreme Court interpreted the Free Speech Clause of the First Amendment as a limitation on federal governmental authority *only*. It had not yet begun using the provision to limit the authority of individual state governments. (Remember the First Amendment says that "*Congress* [emphasis added] shall make no law . . . abridging the freedom of speech . . ."; it says nothing about prohibiting the states from passing laws limiting a citizen's free speech.) In fact, in 1922, the Supreme Court wrote that "neither the 14th Amendment nor any other provision of the Constitution of the United States imposes upon the states any restrictions about 'freedom of speech' . . ."[5]

It was only after this date, in 1925, that the Supreme Court, in the case of *Gitlow* v. *New York*, began to apply the First Amendment to the States.[6] The *Gitlow* case said, in part:

> [F]reedom of speech and of the press—which are protected by the 1st Amendment from abridgment by Congress—are among the fundamental personal rights and 'liberties' protected by the due process clause of the 14th Amendment from impairment by the states."[7]

Even after the idea of protection of free speech

19

against state intrusion became clearer, the application of the First Amendment remained uncertain. Over the next several years, the "clear and present danger" test of Justice Holmes was applied in some cases but not in others. The test was rejected in 1925 in *Gitlow* v. *New York*.[8] This case attempted to further interpret clear and present danger by limiting its application to cases in which a defendant's "speech" violated a law that punished actions.

The "clear and present danger" test had first been stated by Justice Holmes in the *Schenck* case in 1919. The Supreme Court used it in later cases where the Court had to balance the interests of the government against the competing interests of an individual. Even today, a court has to decide which interest is more important: the government's interest in preventing the words, or a citizen's interest in saying those words. One Supreme Court Justice, Hugo Black, strongly opposed this requirement for balancing interests. He said that "the men who drafted our Bill of Rights did all the 'balancing' that was to be done in this field."[9] Justice Black meant that if the citizen was doing something that was protected under the First Amendment, then the government could not stop it.

By 1964, it was widely agreed that the First Amendment provided broad protection for citizens wishing to criticize the government. The 1964 case of *New York Times Company* v. *Sullivan* had to do with a Montgomery, Alabama, commissioner who supervised that city's police department.[10] He claimed in a lawsuit that *The New York Times* newspaper had damaged his reputation. According to him, an advertisement in that paper falsely described maltreatment of African-American students by the Montgomery Police Department. This cast a poor reflection on him personally. A jury awarded the commissioner $500,000 in damages. The jury verdict was upheld on an appeal to the Alabama Supreme Court. The case was then appealed to the United States Supreme Court. The Supreme Court ruled that "the Constitution delimits a State's power to award damages for libel in actions brought by public officials against critics of their official conduct."[11] The Court wrote:

> The constitutional guarantees require, we think, a federal rule that prohibits a public official from recovering damages for a defamatory falsehood relating to his official conduct unless he proves that the statement was made with "actual malice"—that is, with knowledge that it was false or with reckless disregard of whether it was false or not."[12]

This meant that a government official, such as a police commissioner, could not sue a person for complaining about the official's actions. In an article about this case, one constitutional scholar has said, "The central meaning of the [First] Amendment is that seditious libel [criticism of the government] cannot be made the subject of government sanction."[13] In other words, this is the very point of the Free Speech Clause of the First Amendment. The government cannot punish a person for merely complaining about the government.

Brandenburg v. *Ohio*, decided in 1969, was another important case.[14] It involved the boundaries between free speech and unlawful speech. In that case, a Ku Klux Klan leader was convicted under an Ohio law for speaking at a rally and supporting violence against ethnic minorities as a means of political change. The Supreme Court reversed the conviction. The First Amendment does not permit a state to forbid "advocacy of the use of force or of law violation, except where such advocacy was directed to inciting or producing imminent lawless action and was likely to incite or produce such action."[15] In other words, the government cannot stop anyone from talking about using violence against the government, as long as the person is just talking. The government can, however, stop a person from trying to get other people to use violence.

Many Supreme Court cases have dealt with the difference between speaking words in favor of a political change and speaking words that actually

This is believed to be the first flag of the United States Marines and of the Continental Army. The words and the rattlesnake emblem conveyed an important message to England about the American colonies: Leave us alone!

encourage action against the government. A similar and equally important question has been discussed in Supreme Court cases: When does a person's action equal "speech." For example, is using American Sign Language entitled to the same legal protection as spoken words? Or is that what Justice Black called "mere conduct" which is not entitled to free-speech protection?

Justice Black wrote about this dilemma over a definition of speech. He believed that the First Amendment forbade any government restriction on "speech." He also believed, however, that it allowed the government to regulate 'conduct.' He based this view on the inherent danger that arises, in some circumstances, out of violent or controversial conduct. One's actual spoken words then are protected by the First Amendment. Conduct other than mere words, however, is not entitled to the same constitutional protection. Even Justice Black, however, recognized the difficulty in distinguishing between speech and conduct. In *Giboney* v. *Empire Storage and Ice Co.*, decided in 1949, the Justice wrote that several union picketers had violated a law against interfering with buying and selling. The signs they carried urged an ice distributor not to sell ice to non-union peddlers. Justice Black believed that their activity was against the law even though their actions were "carried out by means of language."[16]

In some cases the government argued that a person's words were illegal because they created a breach of the peace. A breach of the peace occurs when the public peace and order is disturbed. Public fights or riots are breaches of the peace. In another case, *Cohen* v. *California* in 1971, a defendant was convicted of breach of the peace for visiting a courthouse while wearing a jacket that had on it a slogan critical of the United States' requirement that young men serve in the military. The Supreme Court overturned the conviction. It said that the defendant's slogan was the type of "speech" protected by the First Amendment. Justice Black agreed with Justice Blackmun, who dissented from the majority opinion of the Court. He insisted that the defendant's "antic . . . was mainly conduct and little speech," and therefore that the conviction should have been allowed to stand.[17]

The current understanding of "free speech" has developed largely in the last half of the twentieth century. Constitutional speech is no longer defined as merely spoken or written words. It also covers a range of expression. Some types do not include the use of words at all. The current explanation of free-speech protection extends beyond mere words. It also covers conduct and action. It is now understood that the First Amendment protects conduct that is "sufficiently imbued with elements of communication."[18] In other words, the First Amendment protects what a person *does* (even when it is "offensive or disagreeable") if the main purpose of the action is to communicate or express an idea. In the Supreme Court's words, the test for determining whether one's conduct is the kind of "speech" that the First Amendment protects is whether there is an "intent to convey a particularized message [and] the likelihood . . . that the message would be understood by those who reviewed it."[19] Furthermore, the current interpretation of the Free Speech Clause includes the legal right to express ideas that are unpopular, extreme, or offensive.

The Supreme Court has also declared some specific nonverbal acts to be protected by the Free Speech Clause. In 1964, a group of African Americans held a "silent and reproachful" sit-in at a public library to protest racial segregation.[20] The State of Louisiana arrested the protestors. They had violated a law making it a criminal offense to gather in a public building and to refuse to move when ordered to do so by an authority. Their conviction was appealed. The Supreme Court declared that the right to protest peaceably, as long as there is no breach of peace, is guarded by the First

Amendment. In 1968, three public school students wore black armbands to school to protest the war in Vietnam.[21] The school, however, had prohibited this conduct on threat of suspension. The Supreme Court held that wearing the armbands was "akin to 'pure speech'" and therefore was protected by the First Amendment.[22] The students could not be suspended from school for wearing the armbands.

When Joey Johnson's case reached the Supreme Court in 1989, the Court used something called O'Brien's test to help it to decide the government's interest in regulating expressive conduct under the First Amendment. O'Brien's test comes from *United States* v. *O'Brien*, a 1968 United States Supreme Court case.[23] During the 1960s and early 1970s the federal Selective Service Act or "draft" ordered all young men of specific ages to register with the government to serve in the military. The young men were given registration certificates called draft cards. The cards contained information about each young man. The government then drafted, or selected, young men to serve in the military from a list of registered men. There were protests in the United States against the war and against the draft. During one of the protests, a young man named O'Brien burned his draft card in front of a crowd. O'Brien was convicted of violating a federal law, since it was a crime to knowingly destroy or mutilate a draft card. His case eventually went to the Supreme Court. O'Brien argued that the law he was convicted of violating was unconstitutional because the act of burning his draft card was "symbolic speech." As such, it was protected by the First Amendment. The Supreme Court did not agree with him. Even if a person engages in an action that communicates an idea, the conduct will not necessarily be protected by the First Amendment. The Court wrote that the government has greater power to limit a person's speech when the speech consists partly of action. The Court used the following test:

> [A] government regulation is sufficiently justified if [1] it is within the constitutional power of the government; [2] it furthers an important or substantial government interest, [3] the governmental interest is unrelated to the suppression of free expression; and [4] the incidental restriction on alleged First Amendment freedoms is no greater than is essential to the furtherance of that interest.[24]

The Supreme Court held that the law prohibiting a person from burning his draft card passed this test and O'Brien's conviction was upheld.

In this country, then, free speech has had its ups and downs. At one time, the federal government could put a person in jail for merely speaking words that were critical of the United States or its leaders. Today, we can freely criticize our government without fear of governmental reaction. Also, today, the Free Speech Clause protects not only spoken words but actions as well. Actions are protected when they are intended to express an idea, and the expression of that idea is more important than the government's interest in regulating the specific conduct. An example of this kind of "speech" is wearing an armband to protest a war. But there are also important government interests at stake and important limits on actions that express ideas. When Joey Johnson burned an American flag in 1984, he believed that he had a Constitutional right to do so. What did the Justices on the Supreme Court think?

3

The Early Legal History of Flag Burning

In the late 1800s there was a movement across the country to pass laws to protect the American flag. Called "flag-desecration" laws, they made it a crime to desecrate, or show disrespect for, the American flag. In those days there was little concern about flag-desecration laws violating a person's free speech rights under the First Amendment. The Supreme Court had not related free-speech claims to conduct at that early time, nor had it applied the limitations of the First Amendment to the states. However, it was not long before state court rulings began striking down the state flag-desecration laws.

Many of the state laws sought to prohibit the use of

the flag for advertising or commercial use, because it was seen as demeaning to the nation's symbol of freedom. The laws were controversial, however. An Illinois law imposed a fine on anyone whose commercial product had a picture of an American flag on it. The law awarded one-half of the fine to the person who turned in the violator. More than one thousand flag-desecration cases were prosecuted in the city of Chicago in less than four months. In 1899 a local Chicago judge ruled that the law was unconstitutional because of the informer fee. The judge even went beyond this ruling. He stated that, in his opinion, it was not a desecration of the flag to use it in advertising.

A second Chicago case was more important because of the grounds on which the case was decided. In *Ruhstrat* v. *People* in 1900, two cigar merchants were convicted in a Chicago court of using a picture of the American flag on cigar box labels. The Illinois Supreme Court, however, held that a business "had a right to advertise in any legitimate manner" and was permitted to use pictures of the American flag in its advertising. The Court also pointed out that the State of Illinois had powers to enact laws related only to the "public health or comfort, the safety or welfare."[1] So, it was powerless to prevent a merchant from placing a picture of an American flag on an advertising label. Furthermore, the

The first ten amendments to the United States Constitution, collectively known as the Bill of Rights, guarantee important individual legal rights to Americans. The Free Speech Clause of the First Amendment says, "Congress shall make no law . . . abridging the freedom of speech."

Court did not believe that using the flag for advertising purposes was necessarily disrespectful of the flag. The conviction was overturned.

About five years later in Colorado, a labor leader was arrested. He had printed a pamphlet that contained a drawing of an American flag and asked the question, "Is Colorado in America?" He had printed the pamphlets during a 1904 labor strike by the Western Federation of Miners. The strikers protested certain arrests and certain actions of the state of Colorado. The charges against the labor leader were ultimately dropped when he produced many other advertisements and circulars that were not against the law but also contained likenesses of the United States flag. The same year a case in Boston, Massachusetts, ruled that the use of a flaglike pattern in an advertisement was not a United States flag, and thus did not violate that state's flag-desecration law.

In 1906, in New York, another case arose involving the use of the flag in another cigar advertisement. The New York Court of Appeals ruled that the desecration law was unconstitutional. The legislature had exceeded its lawful authority by destroying "property rights" of the merchants. Certain manufactured items that had already been made were outlawed. But, most importantly, the court recognized the power of the government to prohibit physical flag desecration or mutilation.

The next year, 1907, the view of the flag-desecration laws of the states changed significantly after a United States Supreme Court case. In *Halter* v. *Nebraska*, two businesses had sold beer that had the brand name "Stars and Stripes" and a picture of an American flag on the label.[2] The businesses were convicted of violating Nebraska's flag-desecration law and were fined fifty dollars. They appealed to the Nebraska Supreme Court. On appeal, the State of Nebraska argued that using the American flag for advertising beer was unpatriotic. Nebraska's Supreme Court claimed that it had the power to prohibit the use of the nation's symbol in advertising. The court said that "patriotic sentiment for the flag and for the noble institutions it symbolizes is outraged by the appearance of the national emblem on a bottle of beer."[3] It also argued that the use of the flag on a bottle of beer would "incite indignant citizens to commit a breach of the peace." It would cause a viewer, especially a soldier who had fought for the country, to "smash the sign."[4] The Nebraska Supreme Court upheld the convictions and the case was appealed to the United States Supreme Court. The nation's highest court, in an 8–1 vote, ruled that the Nebraska law was valid. The Court held that the state had legitimate authority to prohibit desecration of the American flag. It wrote:

> One who loves the Union will love the state in which he resides, and love both of the common country and of the state will diminish in proportion as respect for the flag is weakened.[5]

The Court believed that using the American flag for advertising:

> . . . tends to degrade and cheapen the flag in the estimation of the people, as well as to defeat the object of maintaining it as an emblem of national power and national honor. And we cannot hold that any privilege of American citizenship or that any right of personal liberty is violated by . . . forbidding the flag to be used as an advertisement on a bottle of beer.[6]

In its decision, which would support the state's arguments in the *Johnson* case, the Court asserted that the flag is:

> . . . the symbol of the nation's power—the emblem of freedom in its truest, best sense. It is not extravagant to say that to all lovers of the country it signifies government resting on the consent of the governed; liberty regulated by law; the protection of the weak against the strong; security against the exercise of arbitrary power; and absolute safety for free institutions against foreign aggression.[7]

The *Halter* case remained the most significant ruling on the constitutionality of flag-desecration laws for the next eighty years. It was cited in many other flag-desecration cases and supported many convictions.

In 1918, a Kansas man was convicted of violating the Kansas flag law. He uttered a "very vulgar and indecent use of the flag" in a blacksmith's shop.[8] The Kansas Supreme Court upheld the conviction. The court said that the man did not have the proper respect for the flag. In another case, a Montana man refused to follow a mob's demands that he kiss the flag. The man said, "What is this thing anyway? Nothing but a piece of cotton with a little paint on it and some other marks in the corner there. I will not kiss that thing. It might be covered with microbes."[9] He was convicted of the crime of sedition (encouraging others to rebel against the government) because of the things he said about the flag. Although the court did not quote the state law, apparently the Montana lawmakers believed that not showing respect for the flag was equal to encouraging rebellion against the government. The man had to pay a five-hundred-dollar fine and was sentenced to ten to twenty years at hard labor. A federal judge who reviewed the case called the sentence "horrifying." However, the judge also said that under the *Halter* decision, the Montana law was clearly constitutional.

In 1942, the Arkansas Supreme Court upheld the conviction of a man, ironically named Joe Johnson. He was convicted for publicly exhibiting contempt for the American flag. A welfare officer asked Johnson to salute the flag. She had heard rumors that he would not do it. Johnson said that he would rather die than salute the flag. He told the people in the welfare office, "You can't get anything in here unless you salute the flag. It don't have eyes and can't see, and has no ears and can't hear, and no mouth and can't talk. It doesn't mean nothing to me. It is only a rag."[10]

That same year a similar case occurred in Maine. In *State* v. *Peacock,* a man was convicted under Maine's flag-protection law. Peacock had said, "What is the flag anyway? It is nothing more than a piece of rag. If I had an American flag here now I would strip it up and trample it under my feet."[11] Then he had acted out tearing an imaginary flag and stomping on it. He was found guilty in the trial court. The appellate court, however, overturned his conviction. He had done his acts in his private home and not in public, as required by the statute.

It is interesting to note that these cases all involved words of contempt only; no physical desecration occurred. Negative comments about the flag, without physical violence, were a special exception to the First Amendment right to free speech.

After *Halter,* the United States Supreme Court had

several opportunities to review flag-related conduct. Some of the decisions were related not only to flag desecration but also to actions that did not show respect for the flag. In 1940 in the case of *Minersville School District* v. *Gobitis*, the United States Supreme Court upheld the legality of expelling a ten-year-old child and a twelve-year-old child from school when they refused to salute the flag.[12] This and similar cases arose with members of a religious group called the Jehovah's Witnesses. Their group held religious convictions that kept them from saluting national flags.

In 1943, however, the Supreme Court decided the case of *West Virginia State Board of Education* v. *Barnette*, which overruled the *Gobitis* decision.[13] This case struck down mandatory school flag salute and Pledge of Allegiance requirements. The Court believed that children could not be forced to express a particular opinion. In many ways, the *Barnette* case sets the foundation for the *Texas* v. *Johnson* case. The *Barnette* Court said:

> Those who begin coercive [forced] elimination of dissent soon find themselves exterminating dissenters. Compulsory unification of opinion achieves only the unanimity of the graveyard. . . .
>
> If there is any fixed star in our constitutional constellation, it is that no official, high or petty, can prescribe what shall be orthodox in politics, nationalism, religion or other matters of opinion. . . .[14]

The American flag represented freedom to these prisoners of war who were rescued by Allied troops at Aomori Camp, near Yokohama, Japan, in 1945.

The *Barnette* case continued the Court's move toward greater freedom of individual expression. An even earlier example of this move was the *Stromberg* v. *California* case in 1931.[15] That case was called a "red flag" prosecution. "Red flags" were flags that represented political revolution. This case first declared that symbolic speech was protected by the First Amendment. It held that flags, such as "red flags," could be used to express political ideas.

Up to the day Joey Johnson burned an American flag in Dallas, the United States Supreme Court had never considered the precise legal issue of whether the Free Speech Clause protects a person who burns an American flag in a protest.

4

Flag Burning in the 1960s and 1970s

Before World War I, the focus of court cases involving flag desecration had been advertising and political campaigns. The use of the American flag in advertising rose, however, during and between the two world wars. There was apparently no serious disagreement from the public, patriotic groups, or the government about using the flag in advertising. Following World War I, however, the focus of flag protection began to be centered on its use in political dissent.

In 1917, before the United States entered World War I, a clergyman and others burned an American flag and flags of other countries in a large kettle that was labeled "Melting Pot." A crowd sang hymns and called for international brotherhood. The clergyman, Bouck White, was the head of the Church of the Social Revolution. White and the others who were prosecuted with him claimed that they were not being disloyal to the American flag. They insisted that they were standing for the brotherhood of all mankind. The trial court found White and the others guilty of flag desecration. White was sentenced to thirty days in jail and ordered to pay a one-hundred-dollar fine. At his sentencing, the judge asked him, "Why don't you go off and live in some other country?"[1] His case did not go to the Supreme Court.

With the Vietnam War era of the 1960s and 1970s new flag-desecration cases appeared before the United States Supreme Court. The Court was now applying the First Amendment to state laws as well as federal laws. Citizens found new freedom to express unpopular ideas. When the United States introduced ground combat troops into Vietnam in the early 1960s, the stage was set for strong opposition to the war. Flag burnings became more common, but continued to stir the emotions of politicians and the American people. These emotions reached the highest level of government: President Lyndon Johnson ground his teeth as he looked down on flag-burning protestors from his White House window.[2] The flag burnings increased and prosecutions followed.

The United States flag was used by the federal government for promoting food production and conservation during World War I.

In 1966, a former soldier who had been awarded a bronze star for heroism in World War II was arrested for burning an American flag. Sidney Street burned the flag when he learned that a civil-rights activist, James Meredith, had been shot by a sniper in Mississippi. Street said, "We don't need no damn flag."[3] When a police officer asked if the burning flag was his, Street replied, "Yes; that is my flag; I burned it. If they let that happen to Meredith we don't need an American flag."[4] Street was tried and convicted under a New York flag-desecration law that made it illegal to "mutilate, deface, defile, or defy, trample upon or cast contempt" upon the American flag "either by words or act." On appeal to New York's highest court, the court said that the state had legitimate authority to prevent a breach of peace and prevent flag burning. The conviction was upheld. Street appealed to the United States Supreme Court. Street's lawyers emphasized that his action was clearly a political protest. As such, it was free speech and was protected by the First Amendment to the United States Constitution. In a 5–4 decision, the Supreme Court overturned Street's conviction. But the Court did not decide the central issue of the right to burn a flag as protected free speech. The formal charge against Street and the trial evidence did not prevent the possibility that Street had been convicted solely because of his *verbal* criticism of the flag. The majority opinion rested upon the *Stromberg* red-flag and the *Barnette* flag-salute cases. One may not be convicted solely for verbal criticism of the United States flag. Thus the Court held that Street's criticisms were clearly protected under the First Amendment.

April 15, 1967, in Central Park in New York City was an eventful day. Nearly two hundred thousand people were attending an antiwar, flag-burning rally there. Photographs of the flag burning appeared in the national press and caused concern among members of Congress. In congressional debates, one congressman said:

> I am sure most of us know of the incident in New York's Central Park, on April 15, when thousands witnessed that disgraceful act of a group which publicly burned an American flag.
>
> This repugnant display turned many stomachs, and to add to its revulsion, it was seen by millions of people throughout the world in news photos and telecasts. What was most appalling was the fact that the perpetrators went unpunished.[5]

These congressional debates led to the 1968 enactment of the first federal flag-desecration law. Later, Stephen Radich, owner of a New York City art gallery, was arrested after displaying artwork that protested the Vietnam War. The American flag was displayed in several ways that were thought to be disrespectful. In one sculpture, a stuffed flag was shaped in the form of a dead person hanging from a noose. Radich was found guilty of violating the New York flag-desecration law. He was sentenced to a five-hundred-dollar fine or sixty days in jail. The New York City Criminal Court cited the Supreme Court's *Halter* decision. It said that the First Amendment to the Constitution did not include "a license to desecrate the flag."[6] The court said that the law was properly within the state's police power to outlaw acts that created an "immediate threat to public safety, peace, or order."[7] Radich's conviction was upheld on appeal in New York's intermediate appellate court and in New York's highest criminal court. The state's highest court said that the purpose behind the law was to prevent a breach of the peace; therefore, the law was valid. The case was appealed to the United States Supreme Court.

During oral arguments before the Supreme Court, Radich's lawyers emphasized again the political purpose behind Radich's actions. They claimed that the First Amendment protected Radich's right to political dissent. This included the right to display a flag in a manner that expresses a political idea. The state's rebuttal was that the First Amendment protected only speech and that the use of an American flag was not speech. In 1971 the Supreme Court issued a 4–4 ruling (one Justice did not participate) without a written opinion. When there is a tie vote, under Supreme Court rules, the lower court's ruling is upheld. Thus, Radich's conviction was upheld.

Cases followed in the state and federal courts in which the government claimed that the American flag was treated disrespectfully. The cases included prosecutions for actions such as burning a flag, wearing a flag patch, wearing a flag fashioned into a garment, superimposing peace symbols over the flag, and other expressions similar to the Radich art exhibit. During the Vietnam War era, all such actions were subject to prosecution. State interests were claimed to be more important than a citizen's right to free speech. Such interests were defined as follows: (1) The laws were necessary to protect the flag as the symbol of our nation, and (2) Allowing flag desecration would lead to a breach of the peace. The defendants in those cases, however, generally relied upon the right to free speech that is guaranteed in the First Amendment. Free speech meant something broader than mere verbal expression.

In 1967 Valarie Goguen, a Canadian man, was arrested in Massachusetts for wearing an American flag patch on the seat of his pants. The Massachusetts law imposed a fine against "Whoever publicly mutilates, tramples upon, defaces or treats contemptuously the flag

The caption on this United States Department of Education photo reads, "Flag-raising ceremonies in connection with the observance of patriotic holidays are an important part of the training in citizenship in the Berkeley Public Schools."

of the United States . . ."[8] Goguen said that he did not know that it was against the law to wear the patch. In a trial before a judge, Goguen was convicted and sentenced to one year in jail. When Goguen exercised his right to a jury trial, he was again convicted, but his sentence was reduced to six months. The conviction was reversed in the federal district court, and the case eventually reached the United States Supreme Court. In a 5–4 decision, the Supreme Court said that the "treats contemptuously" phrase of the law under which Goguen was convicted was unconstitutionally vague. It allowed "policemen, prosecutors, and juries to pursue their personal predilections [use their own judgment]."[9] The Court believed that the law did not properly let the public know exactly which actions were wrong so that the actions could be avoided. The Court refused to decide whether wearing a flag patch on the seat of one's pants is protected speech under the First Amendment. The only other flag-desecration case during this time that resulted in a Supreme Court decision before the *Johnson* case was *Spence* v. *Washington*.[10] Harold Spence was arrested in 1970 for displaying a flag with black plastic tape in the shape of a peace symbol in his apartment window. Spence said that the display was a political protest.

> I felt there had been so much killing and that this was not what America stood for. I felt that the flag stood

for America and I wanted people to know that I thought America stood for peace.[11]

Spence was convicted in the lower court under the State of Washington's "improper use" flag law. When Spence's case reached the United States Supreme Court, it held, in a 6–3 opinion, that the Washington flag-desecration law violated Spence's First Amendment rights. The *Spence* case did not hold, however, that a person has an absolute right to treat the flag in any manner that he or she chooses. The Supreme Court's reasoning was very specific to the facts that Spence had altered his own flag, the flag was on private property, and there was no threat to a breach of the peace. The Court also said that it was important that Spence did not permanently disfigure the flag or destroy it. Two parts of the *Spence* opinion would later be important in the *Johnson* flag-burning case. First, the Court recognized that using an American flag in symbolic protest could be a form of "expression." Second, the Court rejected the argument of the State of Washington that the law was valid so long as Spence had other ways of expressing his ideas.

Between 1969 and 1985, the United States Supreme Court refused to hear more than a dozen cases involving flag desecration. These cases involved actions such as wearing a cutout flag as a vest, tearing a flag, burning a flag, and wearing a flag patch on one's pants. A person convicted under a state law does not automatically have a legal right to have his or her case reviewed by the Supreme Court. The Supreme Court meets at the beginning of and periodically during each term, to determine which cases it will decide among the thousands it reviews. It selects only about 2 percent of the cases for a hearing and decision.

At the time of the *Johnson* case, there was a federal flag-desecration law. There were also laws in forty-eight of the fifty states aimed at prohibiting disrespect for the flag. Among the federal appeals courts there were conflicting decisions on whether burning an American flag was a protected free-speech right. In *U.S.* v. *Kime* in 1982, the Fourth Circuit Court of Appeals held that flag burning was not protected speech under the First Amendment.[12] However, the Eleventh Circuit Court of Appeals, in 1984, held that flag burning (when done as speech) was a protected right under the First Amendment.[13] What was clear was that flag allegiance could not be demanded, and pure verbal criticism of the flag was also permitted. Whether burning an American flag as a part of a political demonstration was constitutionally protected, however, remained uncertain.

An event that occurred in Chicago in 1989, a short time before the *Johnson* case, and which stirred strong emotions over the United States flag, was argued before the Supreme Court. A student, Scott "Dred" Tyler, presented an art exhibit composed of a large collection of photographs of flag burnings and flag-draped coffins. Visitors to the exhibit saw the written question: "What is the proper way to display the American flag?" A book in which visitors could write their responses was placed in front of the collection. Between the book and the place where the visitors stood lay a flag on the floor. Visitors had to walk across the flag in order to reach the book. The political outcry against the exhibit was immediate and loud. Both the Illinois and the Indiana legislatures passed resolutions condemning it. The Illinois legislature cut off funds to the sponsor of the exhibit. The Chicago city council and the Illinois legislature passed legislation banning placing a flag on the floor. An estimated five thousand people attended one public protest against the exhibit, and President George Bush condemned the exhibit. Just five days before the Supreme Court heard oral arguments in the *Johnson* case, on March 16, 1989, the United States Senate passed an amendment to the 1968 federal flag-desecration law. The amendment, which passed by a vote of 97–0, outlawed placing a flag on the floor. Emotions were running high when the Supreme Court handed down its decision on June 21, 1989.

5

Government Efforts to Protect the Flag

Americans are proud and protective of their constitutional right to free speech. At the same time, there is an American sympathy for the government's right to protect itself and its symbols. After all, we have laws that protect government buildings, historic government monuments and landmarks, and laws that protect the government itself against treason. During times of a military draft, Americans were required to support the flag. They served as soldiers and even died for their country and its symbols. With all of this in mind, it seems clear that the government would have a strong interest in protecting its national symbol of freedom.

The State of Texas made some of these arguments in

American sailors killed in the line of duty are being buried at sea in the midst of World War II. The American flag covers the bodies of the dead before the burial.

Texas v. *Johnson.* The highest Texas court had reversed Johnson's conviction. It held that his conduct was protected by the Free Speech Clause of the First Amendment. The State appealed this decision to the United States Supreme Court. The Supreme Court allowed each side to present written and oral arguments explaining their legal positions. The issue before the Court was whether the law under which Joey Johnson was convicted was constitutional. The law prohibited any intentional desecration or damage to the flag. If the law did not violate the Constitution, then Johnson was guilty. If the law was unconstitutional, however, then there could be no charge against Johnson.

The lawyer for the state of Texas argued before the United States Supreme Court that the state had strong interests to justify Johnson's conviction for flag burning, and it had historical examples for its argument. The lawyer for the state claimed that in this country, there is a history of political dissent. There is also a history of governmental control over individual expression. The lawyer for Texas argued that the state's interests in keeping the peace and protecting the flag were more important than Johnson's interest in expressing his political dissatisfaction. This argument is *key* to understanding the *Johnson* case. It is also the key to any question of an individual's constitutional rights in a court of law. Such rights cannot be violated merely by the action of one person against another person—governmental action must be involved. When someone claims that his or her personal constitutional rights have been violated, he or she is saying that the government has overstepped its lawful bounds of authority. Unfortunately, the validity of the competing interests of government and individual citizens is not always clear. The courts often balance those interests against each other. In *Johnson*, the lawyer for the state of Texas urged two separate interests that she claimed outweighed Johnson's free speech interests as an individual.

Sometimes the government's interest in regulating a person's conduct "can justify incidental limitations on First Amendment freedoms."[1] In *United States* v. *O'Brien*, for example, the Supreme Court opinion said that a law can properly stop a person from expressing an idea in a particular way so long as four conditions are met:

> (1) The lawmaking body must have constitutional authority to make the law. (2) The law must have an important governmental purpose. (3) The purpose of the law must not be to stop a person from speaking out. (4) The law must be only as restrictive as is necessary to carry out the government's proper reason for the law.[2]

First, the lawyer for Texas argued that the state has a strong interest in preventing a breach of the peace. According to the state, Johnson's flag burning was likely to incite such a breach. This argument was based upon two similar ideas. The first is that an expression that is "directed to inciting or producing imminent lawless action and is likely to incite or produce such action" is not entitled to free speech protection.[3] This argument flows from the cases following *Brandenburg* v. *Ohio*, which examined the "clear and present danger" test.[4] This argument says, too, that the state has the power to prevent a citizen's action when there is a clear and present danger that one person's action will incite or produce lawless action by others. One can constitutionally speak out in favor of breaking the law or in favor of using violent means against the government to bring about political or economic changes. This constitutional right, however, does not go so far as to permit a person to actually encourage others to action that is illegal. For example, in *Brandenburg* the Court ruled that it was unconstitutional to convict a Ku Klux Klan leader for merely supporting violence against ethnic minorities as a means of political reform. The Klan member did not encourage others to actually commit violence. In the *Johnson* case, the lawyer for the state of Texas argued that Johnson's action in burning a flag was not mere support. It was actually directed at inciting lawless action and was likely to incite such action. Texas's lawyer said that because burning an

American flag was an emotionally charged event, it could incite lawless action by those around Johnson.

The second idea that the state used to support its argument was that "fighting words," that is, words that are likely to provoke the average person to fight back, are not protected by the First Amendment. The "fighting words" concept originated from the Supreme Court's decision in *Chaplinsky* v. *New Hampshire*.[5] In *Chaplinsky*, a Jehovah's Witness started a fight with an official by allegedly calling him certain offensive names. Chaplinsky was convicted. A state law forbade a person to address "any offensive, derisive or annoying word to any other person who is lawfully in any street or other public place." The law had been interpreted by the state court to ban only "such words, as ordinary men know, are likely to cause a fight. . . ." A unanimous Supreme Court upheld Chaplinsky's conviction. However, the Court limited its opinion to circumstances in which defendants used hostile words. The Court did not address any other forms of speech. In *Johnson*, the lawyer for Texas argued that Johnson's actions and words were "fighting words" that could have caused the average onlooker to fight back against Johnson. This would cause a breach of peace. The state's claim was that because fighting words are not protected as free speech, Johnson's conviction was lawful.

The lawyer for Texas also claimed that state interests

outweighed individual interests for another reason. The state has "an interest in preserving the flag as a symbol of nationhood and national unity."[6] During oral arguments the following exchange occurred between Justice Antonin Scalia and Kathi Alyce Drew, the attorney for Texas:

> **Scalia:** What is the juridical category you're asking us to adopt in order to say we can punish this kind of speech? Just an exception for flags? It's just a—there's just a flag exception of the First Amendment?

> **Drew:** To a certain extent, we have made that argument in our brief. With respect to the symbolic speech standard, we believe that there are compelling state interests that will in a balancing posture override this individual's symbolic speech rights, and that preserving the flag as a symbol, because it is such a national property, is one of those.[7]

Texas's flag-desecration law restricted the content of Johnson's political expression. Content-based laws like this one are often overbroad and are even censoring in their effect on an individual's expression. The Supreme Court is required to review such laws with "the most exacting scrutiny."[8] The state of Texas disagreed with Johnson's underlying message. It was not just *anything* that he was burning. It was the American flag. Because Johnson did this as a means of expressing his political dissatisfaction, his act was subject to "the most exacting scrutiny" by the Court. Texas, however, had the burden of proving to the Court that its state interests were so

A group of patriotic women are shown hand-sewing an American flag.

important that they should come before and prohibit Johnson's expression of his ideas. The State of Texas believed it had met this high standard of proof. The flag is a unique and special symbol of nationhood and national unity. As such, it deserves protection. Texas's lawyer argued that poor treatment of the flag "may be prohibited because such acts cast doubt on the ideas that nationhood and national unity are the flag's symbols or that national unity actually exists."[9] Again, there were historical precedents. The view that the government could encourage patriotic ideas had been stated expressly in *Halter* v. *Nebraska* in 1907—nearly eighty years before Johnson's actions. But the Supreme Court Justices did not look back only eighty years. They wanted to determine what the Founding Fathers may have had in mind about the First Amendment:

> **O'Connor:** Do you suppose Patrick Henry and any of the Founding Fathers ever showed disrespect to the Union Jack [the British flag]?
>
> **Drew:** Quite possibly, Your Honor.
>
> **O'Connor:** You think they had in mind then in drafting the First Amendment that it should be a prosecutable offense?
>
> **Drew:** Of course, Your Honor, one has no way of knowing whether it would be or not.
>
> **Scalia:** I think your response is that they were willing to go to jail, just as they were when they signed the Declaration [of Independence].

Court: They were hoping they wouldn't get caught. (laughter)

Drew: Yes, Your Honor. I believe the classic line is: "We hang together or separately."

Court: That's right.[10]

So, the question remains: What government limitations on speech are valid? The cases discussed so far have been examined in light of the content of the speaker's message. The First Amendment offers broad protection to citizens speaking out against the government. Although what a person says (the content) may have protection under the First Amendment, the government may lawfully restrict *when*, *where*, and *how* that message may be communicated. These conditions are often called "time, place, and manner restrictions." Some case examples follow.

In *Kovacs* v. *Cooper* in 1949, the Supreme Court upheld a Trenton, New Jersey, law that prohibited the use of "any device known as a sound truck, loud speaker, or sound amplifier . . . which emits therefrom loud and raucous noises and is attached to and upon any vehicle operating or standing upon" public streets or other public places.[11] The Court said that the ordinance prohibiting loud and raucous noises in public was valid. Although city streets are a normal place for the exchange of ideas by speech, how a person speaks is not beyond any lawful governmental control.

In *Cox* v. *Louisiana* in 1965, the leader of a civil rights group was arrested for violating the Louisiana law that forbade a person to "wilfully obstruct the free, convenient and normal use of any public sidewalk, street, highway, bridge, alley, road, or other passageway . . . by impeding, hindering, stifling, retarding or restraining traffic or passage thereon or therein."[12] The leader was convicted in the lower court, but the Supreme Court reversed the conviction. The law permitted some meetings and parades that obstructed traffic, upon approval from the local authorities.

The *Cox* case said that the government could limit free speech activity in public streets. Public places on public property, however, are generally considered to be available for the exercise of free speech, for example:

> Wherever the title of streets and parks may rest, they have immemorially been held in trust for the use of the public and, time out of mind, have been used for purposes of assembly, communicating thoughts between citizens, and discussing public questions. Such use of the streets and public places has, from ancient times, been a part of the privileges, immunities, rights, and liberties of citizens.[13]

The clearest statement of justified governmental limitations on a person's free speech was made by

Justice Hugo Black. He wrote a dissenting opinion in 1969 in *Tinker* v. *Des Moines School District*, the black armband case.[14] Justice Black wrote, "It is a myth to say that any person has a constitutional right to say what he pleases, where he pleases, and when he pleases."[15] The *Kovacs* and *Cox* cases show that there are valid time, place, and manner restrictions that may limit a person's freedom of expression under the First Amendment. These limitations are in addition to the important categories of speech discussed elsewhere, such as "fighting words."

In *Johnson* the state of Texas sought to go past mere time, place, and manner restrictions. It sought to prohibit the act of political dissent itself. Texas claimed that the flag law was valid and that Johnson's action breached the peace. His actions were unprotected "fighting words," and the government had a significant interest in protecting the American flag as a "symbol of nationhood and national unity." Texas's ultimate argument was that preventing a breach of the peace and preserving the symbol of the American flag were more important than allowing Johnson to express his political displeasure by destroying the flag.

Time, place, and manner restrictions did not play a direct role in *Texas* v. *Johnson*. An understanding of those limitations, however, is necessary to understand

"Old Glory" has often been exhibited to promote patriotism in American citizens. Here, peach stones were collected for producing gas masks in World War I.

the right to free speech. In *United States* v. *Eichman*, the major flag-burning case that followed *Johnson*, the government claimed that the federal flag-burning law was a mere restriction on the manner of expression.[16] The government argued that the Flag Protection Act of 1989 was valid. It restricted the manner of expression but did not directly prohibit the particular content of the message. The government claimed in *Eichman* that time, place, and manner restrictions were important to the question of whether a person may burn a flag as a means of political expression.

6

Johnson's Case: Free Speech and Flag Burning

Joey Johnson's attorney, William Kunstler, responded to the state's arguments. He claimed that Johnson had a First Amendment right to burn an American flag as a method of expressing political disagreement. The state of Texas disagreed, however, with the contention that Joey Johnson's act of burning the flag in Dallas was "expressive conduct" and "sufficiently imbued with elements of communication" (under the *Spence* case) to be protected under the First Amendment. Johnson still had to convince the Justices of the Supreme Court of his claims.

First, Kunstler argued that the Texas flag-burning law was unconstitutional because it was vague and overbroad. The Supreme Court has overturned criminal convictions when the laws under which the persons were convicted were so vague or overbroad as to be unconstitutional. Laws must be clearly stated so that citizens know exactly which specific behavior is unlawful. *Baggett* v. *Bullitt*, decided in 1964, was an example of this.[1] In that case, the Supreme Court invalidated, on the grounds of vagueness, a law that required teachers to take an oath stating that the teacher was not a "subversive person." The term subversive person was so vague that it did not have a clear meaning under the law. Therefore, it was unconstitutional. In 1965 in *Dombrowski* v. *Pfister*, a law requiring the registration of "subversive organizations" was struck down as vague and overbroad.[2] What did the law mean by a subversive organization? Who defines it? Kunstler claimed that the law under which Johnson was convicted was similarly overbroad; it says:

> (a) A person commits an offense if he intentionally or knowingly desecrates:
>> (1) a public monument;
>> (2) a place of worship or burial; or
>> (3) a state or national flag.
>
> (b) For purposes of this section, "desecrate" means deface, damage, or otherwise physically mistreat in a way that the actor knows will seriously offend one or more persons likely to observe or discover his action.

(c) An offense under this section is a Class A misdemeanor."[3]

Johnson's attorney claimed that the words *desecration* and *national flag* were not adequately defined in the law. He quoted from a dictionary to define the word desecrate as meaning "to divest of a sacred character or office, to divert from a sacred purpose, to violate the sanctity of, to profane, the opposite of consecrate."[4] But, he pointed out, the flag is commonly used for advertising purposes. He also noted that the president's wife wore a flag scarf. There were flag bikinis, and there were little cocktail flags that you put into a hot dog or meatball and then throw in the garbage pail.[5]

All of these uses were potentially desecrations. But they were not being prosecuted. A person could step outside the front door of the Supreme Court building and see street vendors selling T-shirts that display the flag in all sorts of ways. Souvenirs in the nation's capital display the American flag on magnets, scarves, clothing, and other items. Flag-covered souvenirs were even available in the shops at the government-funded Smithsonian Institute in Washington, D.C. Attorney William Kunstler also questioned what the law meant by the term "national flag." He pointed out that there are seventeen national flags: in addition to "Old Glory,"

A child's kite, formed using the images of an American flag, is flown at the Washington Monument in Washington, D.C. This kite was flown in an event that was sponsored by the Smithsonian Institution. Before World War I, such use of the American flag may have been thought to be unpatriotic and disrespectful.

there is a presidential flag and a flag for each federal department, for example. Did the law apply to these "national" flags? Was the term national flag so vague and overbroad as to lack a clear meaning? Kunstler argued that it was.

A different example of this law's potential vagueness was noted by the Supreme Court itself. A tired person might be convicted under this law, the Court said, for dragging a flag through the mud, knowing that the conduct might offend someone but without any purpose of expressing an idea. This argument applies to the law on its face. However, the Court elected to respond to Johnson's claim on narrower grounds. The Court examined whether the statute was defectively vague as it applied to political expression only.

Kunstler's second argument was that Texas "lacks 'any state interest whatsoever' in regulating the manner in which the flag may be displayed."[6] The attorney claimed that Johnson was free to display the American flag in any way he wanted, without government interference. This argument attempted to remove the balancing test from the case. The attorney claimed that Johnson's free-speech interests could not be outweighed by competing state interests. There was no competing state interest. What interest could the state have in how Johnson displayed the flag? They had attempted to prevent him from expressing ideas that the government did not like. Johnson knew that his ideas were unpopular. In fact, he intended to convey the unpopular political ideas through expressive conduct. He said:

> The American Flag was burned as Ronald Reagan was being renominated as President. And a more powerful statement of symbolic speech, whether you agree with it or not, couldn't have been made at that time. . . . We had new patriotism and no patriotism.[7]

Johnson believed he was making a powerful political statement against the government and doing so was absolutely protected free speech. In effect, he was saying: "Because of my constitutional right of free speech, I can do whatever I want with the flag, and the government can't stop me." In the oral argument, Johnson's attorney said that this went "to the heart of the First Amendment, to hear things or to see things that we hate tests the First Amendment more than seeing or hearing things that we like. It wasn't designed for things we like. They [things we like] never needed a First Amendment."[8]

In response to the state's argument that burning a flag might result in a breach of the peace, Attorney Kunstler argued that, although some people might have been offended, there was no actual breach of the peace:

The Declaration of Independence, adopted on July 4, 1776, says that all people are "endowed by their Creator with certain inalienable Rights." Among the specific legal rights that the American colonists wanted to protect was the right to speak out freely against the government.

A witness was obviously seriously offended by appellant's conduct because he gathered the burned flag and buried it at his home. Nevertheless so seriously offended, this man was not moved to violence. Serious offense occurred, but there was no breach of the peace, nor does the record reflect that the situation was potentially explosive. One cannot equate serious offense with incitement to breach the peace.[9]

Johnson's claim was that the government could not limit his right to speak out on political issues—even if he did so by burning an American flag, and even if it meant that many people would be offended.

7

The Supreme Court Speaks

On June 21, 1989, the United States Supreme Court delivered its landmark decision. It upheld, by a narrow margin, the Texas Court of Criminal Appeals decision that Johnson could *not* be convicted for burning an American flag as a part of a political demonstration. The Court, in a vote of 5-4, held that Johnson's actions constituted symbolic speech and were protected by the First Amendment. Of the nine Justices, five ruled that Johnson's actions were protected under the First Amendment while four disagreed. A change in a single vote would have changed the outcome of the decision. Justice Brennan wrote for the five-member majority which also included Justices Marshall, Blackmun,

The Justices of the Supreme Court sit in the Supreme Court building in the nation's capitol. In 1989, the Justices decided that Joey Johnson could not be convicted as a criminal for burning an American flag in a political protest.

Scalia, and Kennedy. Chief Justice Rehnquist and Justices White, O'Connor, and Stevens dissented.

The five Justices who formed the majority opinion had widely varying ideas about politics and the law. The majority had a strong view of personal rights of expression that are guaranteed by the Constitution. The five believed that Johnson's act of burning an American flag in the context of a political demonstration "was sufficiently imbued with elements of communication" to be protected by the Free Speech Clause of the First Amendment.[1]

The Court did recognize the state's interest in preventing a breach of the peace. It did not, however, find any facts to apply that interest in this case. Factually, there was no disturbance of the peace. The Court rejected Texas's argument that a mere "potential for a breach of the peace" was adequate to restrict Johnson's right to free expression.[2] Furthermore, Johnson's actions were not "fighting words" that were "likely to provoke the average person to retaliation, and thereby cause a breach of the peace."[3]

In response to the claim of the state's interest in protecting the flag as a symbol of nationhood and national unity, the Court had this to say:

> If there is a bedrock principle underlying the First Amendment, it is that the government may not

prohibit the expression of an idea simply because society finds the idea itself offensive or disagreeable . . . We have not recognized an exception to this principle even where our flag has been involved."[4]

The lawyer for Texas had argued that the state's flag-protection law was valid because the law preserved the flag's symbolism of nationhood and national unity. But the Supreme Court rejected that reason for the law. The Court said that Texas could not support its view of the flag by preventing citizens from expressing ideas that were different from the state's.

The dissenting opinion said that the law did not stop all kinds of protests against the flag. It only stopped destruction of the flag. The dissent said that the law was valid since other kinds of protests, which expressed the same idea, were available to the protestor. The majority opinion believed, however, that if a government may stop specific ways of protesting, then ultimately it would be directing exactly which way a person could express an idea. It refused to allow the government to do that.

The Court concluded its rationale with these words: "We do not consecrate [honor] the flag by punishing its desecration, for in doing so we dilute the freedom that this cherished emblem represents."[5]

The Court did reject William Kunstler's argument

78

that the government has no "state interest whatsoever" in regulating the display of the flag.[6] But the recognition of that interest does not imply a government's right to punish flag burning as a means of political protest.

Justice Kennedy, who was appointed by President Ronald Reagan, wrote a separate concurring opinion. Kennedy recognized the powerful emotions that are held by many citizens for their country's flag. He wrote that "[i]t is poignant but fundamental that the flag protects those who hold it in contempt."[7] He also said, "we must make decisions we do not like. We make them because they are right, right in the sense that the law and the Constitution, as we see them, compel the result."[8]

The Court did not say that all flag burning is protected under the First Amendment. For example, a person can still be convicted of trespassing or vandalism for removing and burning a flag flying over a public building. Johnson's act of burning a flag as a means of political expression was protected free speech since there was no breach of the peace.

The dissenting opinion, written by Chief Justice Rehnquist, presented a passionate and patriotic tribute to the American flag and its colorful history. He quoted famous sayings about the flag, such as Ralph Waldo Emerson's "Concord Hymn":

By the rude bridge that arched the flood
Their flag to April's breeze unfurled,
Here once the embattled farmers stood
And fired the shot heard round the world.[9]

He quoted a long poem entitled "Barbara Frietchie" by John Greenleaf Whittier that celebrates the "Flag of Freedom and Union." He also quoted the entire national anthem.

Chief Justice Rehnquist's dissenting opinion did not rely upon mere emotion and patriotism, however. His opinion also looked to historic precedents. Chief Justice Rehnquist did not believe that flag burning was "speech." He wrote: "flag burning is the equivalent of an inarticulate grunt or roar that, it seems fair to say, is most likely to be indulged in not to express any particular idea, but to antagonize others."[10] The minority reviewed the Court's prior decisions in which it held that a person's freedom of expression is not absolute. For example, in *Chaplinsky* v. *New Hampshire,* a unanimous Court upheld the conviction of a man for cursing and ridiculing a local marshal.[11] The man had been convicted under a state law that made it unlawful to "address any offensive, derisive or annoying word to any other person who is lawfully in any street or other public place."[12] The minority believed that Johnson's action of burning a flag, like Chaplinsky's action of

Chief Justice William Rehnquist of the United States Supreme Court is shown here. Chief Justice Rehnquist wrote the minority opinion in the *Johnson* case. He believed that the flag should be protected as a symbol of nationhood and national unity, and that Johnson should not be permitted to lawfully burn an American flag.

cursing a marshal, was not necessary to express his idea. There were many other forms of expression available to Johnson to make known his opinions against America, without burning a flag. The minority also believed that Johnson's act could have caused onlookers to riot. Since actions that cause others to riot are not protected by the First Amendment, Johnson's actions should not have been protected either. Chief Justice Rehnquist viewed it as ironic that "[t]he government may conscript men into the Armed Forces where they must fight and perhaps die for the flag, but the government may not prohibit the public burning of the banner under which they fight."[13]

Justice Stevens wrote a separate dissenting opinion. He likened the flag to a national memorial that is protected from vandalism. He believed that the state's interest in protecting the flag outweighs an individual's interest in expressing ideas through burning a flag. He too saw it as important that other, less offensive methods, were available to express the same political ideas. He wrote:

> [S]anctioning the public desecration of the flag will tarnish its value—both for those who cherish the ideas for which it waves and for those who desire to don the robes of martyrdom by burning it.[14]

After the decision was handed down by the

Supreme Court, Joey Johnson posed triumphantly with charred American flags. One of his lawyers said about the decision: "If free expression is to exist in this country, people must be as free to burn the flag as they are to wave it."[15]

Although the vote was close, and the result may have been distasteful to many Americans, the decision was clear: Freedom of political dissent is so important that even the United States flag may be desecrated as a means of expressing such dissent.

8

Firestorm of Indignation

During the 1988 presidential campaign, patriotism and respect for the American flag became hot issues. The Democratic candidate was Michael Dukakis, the governor of Massachusetts. Dukakis had vetoed a law requiring daily recitation in public schools of the Pledge of Allegiance to the American flag. He believed that the law was unconstitutional. Because of this veto, George Bush, the Republican presidential candidate and a World War II veteran, questioned Governor Dukakis's loyalty to the flag. During the campaign, Bush often led his audiences in recitation of the Pledge of Allegiance. George Herbert Walker Bush was elected as the president of the United States in November 1988 as the *Johnson* case was making its way through the courts.

The Supreme Court's decision in the *Johnson* case lit

a "firestorm of indignation" in the country.[1] President George Bush responded to the decision by saying, "Flag burning is wrong—dead wrong."[2] Within days of the Court's decision, Bush proposed a Constitutional amendment to overturn the result. Thirty-nine resolutions were sponsored in the United States House of Representatives and Senate to overturn the decision. The Senate approved an attempt to overrule *Johnson* in a vote of 97–3. The House of Representatives passed a resolution by a vote of 411 to 15 that expressed concern over the decision. Sixteen states criticized *Johnson* in their Senates or Houses of Representatives. Politicians all around the country used the *Johnson* decision as an opportunity to publicly exhibit their patriotism and denounce the Court's approval of Joey Johnson's actions. One poll showed that 65 percent of the public disapproved of the ruling.[3] The press took positions on both sides of the issue. Democratic Senator Sam Nunn of Georgia said, "I will join the efforts of other members of Congress in rectifying this action, including supporting a constitutional amendment, if necessary."[4] If Congress did approve a constitutional change, it would have to be sent to the states for approval. Any further Supreme Court decisions would have to be based on the whole Constitution, including the amendment. Seventy-one

President George Bush used the American flag to symbolize his love for the United States. President Bush wanted a constitutional amendment to overrule the *Johnson* decision and prohibit all flag burning.

percent of the American public favored a constitution-al amendment to overrule *Johnson*.[5]

Congress attempted to overrule *Johnson* by passing the Flag Protection Act of 1989.[6] This act penalized anyone who "knowingly mutilates, defaces, physically defiles, burns, maintains on the floor or ground, or tramples upon any flag of the United States." The pur-pose of the Act was:

> . . . to protect the physical integrity of the American flag against mutilating, defacing, burning, trampling upon or maintaining on the floor or ground. The subject matter of this legislation is unique, as the American flag has an historic and intangible value unlike any other symbol.[7]

But the Flag Protection Act did not stop people from burning flags. In fact, more flags were burned to protest the Act. When the cases reached the courts, the new law was struck down as unconstitutional by fed-eral district judges in Seattle, Washington, and Washington, D.C. The judges ruled that (1) the Flag Protection Act was not "content neutral," and (2) according to the *Johnson* case, the Act was an uncon-stitutional limitation on a person's free speech rights under the First Amendment. Both courts held that the law must be judged by the "most exacting scrutiny" as required by *Boos* v. *Berry* because the law suppressed the actor's expressive conduct.[8]

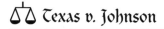

The American flag is flown at half-mast at the United States capitol after the death of a former United States senator. Here, in response to the *Johnson* case, Congress passed the 1989 Flag Protection Act, which criminalized flag desecration. The law was struck down by the Supreme Court as unconstitutional.

The Supreme Court accepted review of new flag-burning cases under an extraordinary provision of the Act that required a speedy review by the Supreme Court. Two cases were consolidated into one case called *U.S. v. Eichman.*[9] In the government's appeal briefs, the government argued two main points to overrule the *Johnson* case. First, the government lawyers claimed that burning an American flag was outside of First Amendment protection in a way similar to other actions, such as defamation and "fighting words," that have never been given constitutional protection. The purpose of those laws, however, was to protect innocent persons. The purpose of the Flag Protection Act was to suppress an unpopular expression of a political opinion. The government argued again, as it did in *Johnson*, that the American flag is a unique symbol of the nation and that as such it is entitled to special treatment. Also, the government's lawyers claimed that the law was "content neutral" because it did not specifically "target expressive conduct on the basis of the content of its message."[10] The government claimed that burning a flag was like speaking too loudly through a loudspeaker on a public street. By this argument, the government was claiming that the Flag Protection Act was more like a valid restriction, one that merely limits the *manner* in which a person may express dissent. (Remember that the government may constitutionally impose reasonable time, place, and manner restrictions on free speech.) The government claimed that burning a flag did not pass the test described in *Spence*, which required a person to deliver a "particularized message."[11] The *Spence* case said that actions are entitled to free-speech protection under the First Amendment when the actions are "sufficiently imbued with elements of communication."[12]

The lawyers for the flag burners said that their clients were entitled to the protection of the First Amendment under the ruling of the *Johnson* case. They claimed that the new flag-burning law, like earlier flag-burning laws, was not "content neutral." Instead, Congress had passed this law for the very purpose of protecting the flag's symbolic value. In effect, then, the very purpose of the law was to suppress a political opinion that opposed that symbol.

In another 5–4 decision, the Supreme Court ruled in *Eichman* in favor of free expression under the First Amendment. The Court was not swayed by the vast popular opposition to flag burning. The Court held that "any suggestion that the government's interest in suppressing speech becomes more weighty as popular opposition to that speech grows is foreign to the First Amendment."[13] The Court was saying that the

Constitution does not change with popular opinion. Constitutional rights are fixed legal rights that are not reduced just because most people do not like either those rights or the way those rights are expressed. The *Eichman* opinion was written by Justice Brennan, who had also written the *Johnson* opinion. *Eichman* supported the principles the Court had set down in *Johnson*. Again, the Court believed that the "most exacting scrutiny" test of *Boos* had to apply because the law was related to the "suppression of free expression" and as such, it would not withstand constitutional scrutiny. The Court rejected any claim that burning a flag was a mere manner of expression that could be prevented under "time, place, and manner" limitations or as "fighting words." The reason that the "time, place, and manner" restrictions did not apply was that the purpose of the law clearly was to suppress the content of a person's speech, not simply the manner of speech.

Once again, the four-member dissenting group emphasized the unique role of the flag and claimed that its symbolic value was more important than the value of allowing a person to burn it as a means of political expression. But this time the dissent was not as colorful or as strong as it had been in the *Johnson* case.

Politicians responded negatively to the decision, but the political outcry was not as great as it was after the

Johnson decision. Congress did consider a constitutional amendment to prohibit flag desecration, but it failed. The Court's decision was firm: A person may, under protection of the First Amendment, burn a flag as a means of expressing political dissent. Within months, the flag-desecration "firestorm" slipped out of the minds of the public and the politicians. Many politicians were outraged by a person burning a flag, and they were willing to pass a law to prohibit that action. They did not, however, favor a limitation to the Bill of Rights that would constitutionally prohibit that action. Even most opponents to flag burning believed that it is more important to allow a person to express an opposing political opinion—no matter how distasteful that opinion might be—than to protect the symbol of freedom from abuse.

9

The Land of the Free and the Home of the Brave

Freedom of speech is one of the defining rights of American citizens. The First Amendment of the Bill of Rights secured to citizens the rights of freedom of religion and freedom of speech. These rights give individuals the freedom to hold unpopular beliefs and opinions that may not be held by the majority of society. People can also openly express those beliefs and opinions without fear of government punishment.

American history celebrates democracy and individualism. The rights in the First Amendment are so strongly held and believed in that many thousands of Americans have died on foreign soil to protect them. The American flag is the symbol behind which many

The American flag is raised at Independence Hall, birthplace of the American Constitution, in Philadelphia, Pennsylvania. The new flag was the symbol of the new nation.

American soldiers have fought for freedom. So, when Joey Johnson burned an American flag outside the Republican National Convention in 1984, many Americans were offended by his actions.

Yet, only in an open and free society that permits expression of ideas can people speak out against society itself. William Kunstler, the attorney who argued the *Johnson* case before the Supreme Court said:

> The solution to racist, hate-filled speech from Klan members, white-supremacists and the like is more speech, not repression of it. That's why we should have the right to burn the flag—which is symbolic speech. If the flag stands for anything, it stands for that right.[1]

From this, one may reason that an appropriate response to flag burning is not repression of it, but more speech. That is, just as there is freedom to burn the flag, there is freedom to speak out against flag burning. Flag burning is not a constitutional right, but free speech is a protected right. It may be exercised symbolically in the form of flag burning.

The *Johnson* case assured Americans that they could publicly express an unpopular idea—even in a potentially offensive manner—without fear of being put in jail.

In June 1996, the Phoenix Art Museum in Phoenix, Arizona, hosted a controversial exhibit on the American

The Declaration of Independence and the Constitution of the United States are revered documents that are kept in the National Archives in Washington, D.C.

flag. It featured eighty works created over the last fifty years. The exhibit, which was titled "Old Glory: The American Flag in Contemporary Art" aimed to show the "use and abuse" of the American flag.[2] Responses to the exhibit were mixed. There were noisy, flag-waving demonstrations, letter-writing campaigns, and threats of legal action. Some people also supported the freedom of expression behind the exhibit. The Phoenix Art Museum, which is supported largely by funding from private citizens, stood behind its decision to house the exhibit.[3]

Although many political leaders were opposed to Joey Johnson's actions, his freedom was protected by the law. Perhaps, at least for this era, the last serious effort to outlaw flag burning ended on December 12, 1995. On that date, the United States Senate failed to pass a constitutional amendment that would have given Congress the power to outlaw flag burning. For now, protection of the flag as the symbol of political freedom does not come before the freedom to express political ideas—even unpopular ideas.

Questions for Discussion

1. Does the Free Speech Clause protect only spoken words?

2. Do you think it is unpatriotic to use an American flag in an advertisement? Why or why not?

3. Do you think it is disrespectful to wear the American flag as an article of clothing? Why or why not?

4. Do you think offensive language should be protected under the Free Speech Clause of the First Amendment? Why or why not?

5. Do you believe the Constitution should be changed in order to prevent a person from burning the American flag? Why or why not?

6. Do you think the government should place legal limits on acceptable and nonacceptable forms of protest? Why or why not?

Chapter Notes

Chapter 1

1. *Texas* v. *Johnson*, 491 U.S. 397, 431 (1989).
2. Ibid., p. 399.
3. Ibid., p. 406.

Chapter 2

1. The Sedition Act, 1 State 596 (1798).
2. *Schenck* v. *United States*, 249 U.S. 47 (1919).
3. Ibid., p. 52.
4. 354 U.S. 298 (1957).
5. *Prudential Insurance Company* v. *Cheek*, 259 U.S. 530, 543 (1922).
6. 268 U.S. 652 (1925).
7. Ibid., pp. 652, 666.
8. Ibid., p. 652.
9. *Konigsberg* v. *California*, 366 U.S. 36 (1961); *Barenblatt* v. *United States*, 360 U.S. 109, 140-144 (1959).
10. *New York Times Co.* v. *Sullivan*, 376 U.S. 254 (1964)
11. Ibid., p. 283.
12. Ibid., pp. 279-280.
13. Harry Kalven, Jr., "The New York Times Case: A note on 'the Central Meaning of the First Amendment,'" *Supreme Court Review*, 1964, pp. 191, 209.
14. 395 U.S. 444 (1969).

15. *Brandenburg* v. *Ohio*, 395 U.S. 444, 447 (1969).

16. *Giboney* v. *Empire Storage and Ice Co.*, 336 U.S. 490 (1949)

17. *Cohen* v. *California*, 403 U.S. 15 (1971).

18. *Spence* v. *Washington*, 418 U.S. 405 (1974).

19. 491 U.S., pp. 410-411.

20. *Brown* v. *Louisiana*, 383 U.S. 131 (1966).

21. *Tinker* v. *Des Moines Independent School District*, 393 U.S. 503, 505 (1969).

22. Ibid., p. 503.

23. 391 U.S. 367 (1968).

24. *United States* v. *O'Brien*, 391 U.S. 367, 377 (1968).

Chapter 3

1. 57 N.E. 41 (Ill. 1990).

2. 205 U.S. 34 (1907).

3. Robert Justin Goldstein, *Saving "Old Glory"* (Boulder, Colo.: Westview Press, 1995), p. 52.

4. Ibid., p. 52.

5. *Halter* v. *Nebraska*, 205 U.S. 34, 42 (1907).

6. Ibid., pp. 42-43.

7. Ibid., p. 43.

8. *State* v. *Shumaker*, 175, 978 (Kan. 1918).

9. *Ex Parte Starr*, 263 F. 145 (D. Mont. 1920).

10. *Johnson* v. *State*, 163 SW2d 153 (Ark. 1942).

11. *State* v. *Peacock*, 25 A.2d 491 (Me. 1942).

12. 310 U.S. 586 (1940).

13. 319 U.S. 624 (1943).

14. Ibid., pp. 631-642.

15. *Stromberg* v. *California*, U.S. 359 (1931).

Chapter 4

1. Robert Justin Goldstein, *Saving "Old Glory"* (Boulder, Colo.: Westview Press, 1995), p. 84.

2. Hugh Sidey, "Giving Honor to Old Glory," *Time*, July 3, 1989, p. 16.

3. *Street* v. *New York*, 394 U.S. 576 (1969).

4. Ibid., p. 579.

5. 113 Congressional Record 16, 476 (1967).

6. *People* v. *Radich*, 53 Misc. 2d 717, New York Criminal Court (1967).

7. Ibid., p. 684.

8. Massachusetts General Laws, p. 264.

9. *Smith* v. *Goguen*, 415 U.S. 566, 575 (1974).

10. Ibid., p. 418

11. *Spence*, p. 408.

12. *U.S.* v. *Kime*, CR-80-95-G, M. District, North Carolina, June 12, 1981 (unpublished); *U.S.* v. *Kime*, No. 81-5160, 4th Circuit, January 28, 1982; *U.S.* v. *Kime*, 459 U.S. 949 (1982).

13. *Monroe* v. *State Court of Fulton County*, 739 F. 2d. 568, 572, 574 (11th Cicuit, 1984).

Chapter 5

1. *United States* v. *O'Brien*, 391 U.S. 367 (1968).

2. Ibid.

3. *Brandenburg* v. *Ohio*, 395 U.S. 444 (1969).

4. Ibid., p. 447.

5. 315 U.S. 568 (1942).

6. *Texas* v. *Johnson*, 491 U.S. 397, 410 (1989).

7. Peter Irons and Stephanie Guitton, eds., *May It Please the Court: The Most Significant Oral Arguments Made Before the Supreme Court Since 1955* (New York: The New Press, 1993), p. 155.

8. *Boos* v. *Berry*, 485 U.S. 312 (1988).

9. *Texas* v. *Johnson*, 491 U.S. 397, 413 (1989).

10. Irons and Guitton, pp. 155-156.

11. 336 U.S. 77 (1949).

12. 379 U.S. 536 (1965).

13. *Hague* v. *C.I.O.*, 307 U.S. 496, 515-516 (1939).

14. 393 U.S. 503 (1969).

15. Ibid., p. 522.

16. 496 U.S. 310 (1990).

Chapter 6

1. 377 U.S. 360 (1964).

2. 380 U.S. 479 (1965).

3. Texas Penal Code Ann. 42.09 (1989).

4. Peter Irons and Stephanie Guitton, eds., *May It Please the Court: The Most Significant Oral Arguments Made Before the Supreme Court Since 1955* (New York: The New Press, 1993), p. 157.

5. Ibid.

6. *Texas* v. *Johnson*, 491 U.S. 397 (1989).

7. 491 U.S. at 406.

8. Irons and Guitton, p. 159.

9. Ibid., p. 158.

Chapter 7

1. *Texas* v. *Johnson*, 491 U.S. 397, 406 (1989).

2. Ibid., p. 409.

3. Ibid.

4. Ibid., p. 414.

5. Ibid., p. 420.

6. Ibid., p. 418.

7. Ibid., p. 421.

8. Ibid., pp. 420-421.

9. Ibid., pp. 397, 422.

10. Ibid., p. 432.

11. 315 U.S. 568 (1942).

12. *Chaplinsky* v. *New Hampshire*, 315 U.S. 568, 569 (1942).

13. 491 U.S. at 435.

14. Ibid., p. 437.

15. Walter Isaacson, "O'er the Land of the Free," *Time*, July 3, 1989, p. 15.

Chapter 8

1. Michael D'Antonio and Richard C. Firstman (Contibuting authors: Laura T. Ryan and Paula Park), "Rallying Round the Flag," *Newsday*, July 2, 1989, p. 4.

2. Walter Isaacson, "O'er the Land of the Free," *Time*, July 3, 1989, p. 15.

3. Tamar Jacoby with Ann McDaniel and Peter McKillop, "A Fight for Old Glory," *Newsweek*, July 3, 1989, p. 18.

4. Ibid.

5. Ibid.

6. 18 USC 700

7. Ibid.

8. 485 U.S. 312 (1988).

9. 496 U.S. 310 (1990).

10. *United States* v. *Eichman*, 496 U.S. 310, 315 (1990).

11. *Spence* v. *Washington*, 418 U.S. 405, 411 (1974).

12. Ibid., p. 409.

13. *United States* v. *Eichman*, 496 US 310, 318 (1990).

Chapter 9

1. William M. Kunstler and Sheila Isenberg, *My Life as a Radical Lawyer* (New York: Birch Lane Press, 1994), p. 368.

2. B. Drummond Ayers, Jr., "Art or Trash? Arizona Exhibit on American Flag Unleashes a Controversy," *The New York Times*, June 8, 1996, p. 6.

3. Ibid.

Glossary

abridge—To reduce. The First Amendment prevents Congress from abridging (reducing) a person's freedom of speech.

appeal—A request to a higher court asking for a review of the lower court's decision.

appellate court—A court that has the authority to review decisions of trial courts.

Bill of Rights—The first ten amendments to the United States Constitution.

breach of the peace—Disturbance of public peace and order.

brief—A document that contains a lawyer's arguments on behalf of a client, that is sent to a court.

clear and present danger—The danger that unlawful action is expected close in time to a person's advocating unlawful action.

communism—A political and social system in which the government forces common ownership of property instead of permitting private ownership of property.

concurring opinion—A judge's legal opinion in an appellate court decision that agrees with the majority opinion, but it is written separately to state special or different reasons for the same result.

Congress—The United States Senate and House of Representatives.

constitution—A document agreed upon by the citizens of a land as the controlling law to which all other laws are subject. It describes the powers and limits of power of the government. In the United States, the United States Constitution is the supreme law of the land.

contempt—A willful disregard of authority.

content—The content of a person's speech is the message of the speech. It is what the person is saying. This is different from how, when, or where the person is saying the message.

content neutral—The government in the *Eichman* case argued that the Flag Protection Act was "content neutral." The law did not prohibit an action based on the "content" or message of what the person was trying to express.

conviction—The result of a criminal trial in which a person is found guilty of a crime.

Declaration of Independence—The document adopted by the Second Continental Congress of the United States on July 4, 1776, that declared that the United States was an independent country and no longer subject to the English Crown.

desecrate—Treat something without respect.

dissenting opinion—A judge's legal opinion in an appellate court decision that disagrees with the majority opinion.

federal courts—Courts that decide cases under the authority of the United States government. State courts exist and decide cases under the authority of state governments.

fighting words—Words that are likely to provoke the average person to retaliation, and thereby cause a breach of the peace. Fighting words are not protected under the Free Speech Clause.

First Amendment—It was adopted in 1791 as a part of the Bill of Rights. It says: "Congress shall make no law respecting an establishment of religion, or prohibiting the free exercise thereof; or abridging the freedom of speech, or of the press; or the right of the people peaceably to assemble, and to petition the Government for a redress of grievances."

Founding Fathers—The political leaders who were important in establishing the United States.

framers—The political leaders who participated in drafting and adopting the United States Constitution.

Free Speech Clause—That part of the First Amendment that protects a person's right to speak out. The Free Speech Clause says: "Congress shall make no law . . . abridging the freedom of speech. . . ."

imminent—Close in time, near at hand.

inalienable rights—Personal rights that cannot be given away by a person or taken from a person by the government.

insubordination—In the military, insubordination is refusal to obey the order of a higher-ranking person.

Jehovah's Witnesses—A religious group whose teachings include refusal to salute the flag and strict pacifism.

Ku Klux Klan—A group that limits its members to white American Protestants and that opposes with violence all other ethnic groups.

libel—To injure a person's reputation in a published writing.

majority opinion—The legal opinion in an appellate court decision that is adopted by most of the judges of that court when not all of the judges agree. The majority opinion is the law of the case. On the Supreme Court, one Justice writes the majority opinion.

minority opinion—The legal opinion in an appellate court decision that is adopted by a minority of judges of that court when not all judges agree. The minority opinion is not law and it is not binding upon anyone, but it does tell why the dissenting judges do not agree with the decision of the majority.

Most Exacting Scrutiny Test—The test explained in the Supreme Court case of *Boos* v. *Berry* that says that a law that attempts to limit what a person says will be subject to the "most exacting scrutiny" of the Court. If a law is not necessary to an important state interest and it is not narrowly drawn to protect that interest, then it does not pass this test. The law will then be struck down as unconstitutional.

O'Brien's Test—The test explained in the Supreme Court case of *United States* v. *O'Brien* that applies when a law prohibits a person's actions that are done as "symbolic speech." To pass this test and to be constitutional the law must (1) be within the constitutional power of the government, (2) further an important or substantial government interest, (3) be unrelated to the suppression of free expression, and (4) make clear the restriction on free speech is not any greater than is necessary to the essential furtherance of the government's interest in the law.

patriotism—Love or devotion for your country.

plunder—Steal.

red flag—A flag of an extreme revolutionary political party.

scrutiny—A close examination.

state interest—Interest of the government in performing its lawful functions.

Supreme Court—The highest court in the United States.

symbolic speech—An act that expresses an idea.

time, place, and manner restrictions—Limitations on when, where, and how a person may communicate.

unconstitutional—Something that is contrary to the Constitution.

venerate—Respect; revere.

Further Reading

Apel, Warren S., ed. *The Flag-Burning Page*. (On the Internet at http://www.indirect.com/www/warren/flag.html) No date.

Goldstein, Robert Justin. *Saving "Old Glory."* Boulder, Colo.: Westview Press, 1995.

Goldwin, Robert A., and William A. Schambra, eds. *How Does the Constitution Secure Rights?* Washington, D.C.: American Enterprise Institute for Public Policy Research, 1985.

Guenter, Scot M. *The American Flag 1777-1924*. Cranbury, N.J.: Associated University Presses, 1990.

Hentoff, Nat. *The First Freedom*. New York: Delacorte Press, 1988.

Kunstler, William M., and Sheila Isenberg. *My Life as a Radical Lawyer*. New York: Birch Lane Press, 1994.

Leone, Bruno, ed. *Free Speech*. San Diego, Calif.: Greenhaven Press, Inc., 1994.

Lieberman, Jethro K. *Free Speech, Free Press, and the Law*. New York: Lothrop Lee & Shepard, 1980.

Mastai, Boleslaw, and Marie-Louise D'Otrange. *Stars and Stripes*. Fort Worth, Tex.: Amon Carter Museum, 1973.

Sedeen, Margaret. *Star-Spangled Banner*. Washington D.C.: National Geographic Society, 1993.

Zeinert, Karen. *Free Speech: From Newspapers to Music Lyrics*. Springfield, N.J.: Enslow Publishers, Inc., 1995.

Index

Kunstler, William, 67, 68, 69, 71, 72, 78, 95

M

Marshall, Thurgood, 75
Meredith, James, 44
Minersville School District v. Gobitis, 38
Montgomery Police Department, 21

N

New York Times v. Sullivan, 21
Nunn, Sam, 85

O

O'Brien, David Paul, 27, 28
O'Connor, Sandra Day, 61, 77

P

Phoenix Art Museum, 95, 97
Publius, 10

R

Radich, Stephen, 45–47
Reagan, Ronald, 5, 8, 72, 79
red flag, 40
Rehnquist, William H., 77, 79, 80, 82
Republican National Convention, 5, 95
Revolutionary Communist Youth Brigade, 6
Revolutionary War, 10
Ruhstrat v. People, 31

S

Scalia, Antonin, 59, 61, 77
Schenck v. United States, 17, 20
Sedition Act of 1798, 16
Selective Service Act, 27
sit-in, 26

Smith Act, 18
Spence, Harold, 49, 50
Spence v. Washington, 49, 50, 67, 90
State v. Peacock, 37
Stevens, John Paul, 77, 82
Street, Sydney, 44
Stromberg v. California, 40, 45
symbolic speech, 8, 28

T

Texas v. Johnson, 8, 35, 38, 49, 50–52, 55–58, 64, 66, 84, 85, 86, 87, 89, 91, 92, 95
time, place and manner restrictions, 62, 64, 66, 90, 91
Tinker v. Des Moines School District, 64
Tyler, Scott "Dred", 52

U

United States v. Eichman, 66, 89, 90, 91
United States v. Kime, 51
United States v. O'Brien, 27, 28, 56

V

Vietnam War, 27, 42, 45, 47

W

Western Federation of Miners, 33
West Virginia State Board of Education v. Barnette, 38, 40, 45
White, Bouck, 42
White, Byron R., 77
Whittier, John Greenleaf, 80
World War I, 41
World War II, 44, 84

Y

Yates v. United States, 18–19